Fast Facts About Dog

Fast Facts About
GERMAN SHEPHERDS

by Marcie Aboff

Raintree is an imprint of Capstone Global Library Limited, a company incorporated in England and Wales having its registered office at 264 Banbury Road, Oxford, OX2 7DY – Registered company number: 6695582
www.raintree.co.uk
myorders@raintree.co.uk

Text © Capstone Global Library Limited 2021
The moral rights of the proprietor have been asserted.
All rights reserved. No part of this publication may be reproduced in any form or by any means (including photocopying or storing it in any medium by electronic means and whether or not transiently or incidentally to some other use of this publication) without the written permission of the copyright owner, except in accordance with the provisions of the Copyright, Designs and Patents Act 1988 or under the terms of a licence issued by the Copyright Licensing Agency, 5th Floor, Shackleton House, 4 Battle Bridge Lane, London SE1 2HX (www.cla.co.uk). Applications for the copyright owner's written permission should be addressed to the publisher.

Edited by Megan Peterson
Designed by Sarah Bennett
Picture research by Kelly Garvin
Production by Tori Abraham
Originated by Capstone Global Library Ltd

978 1 3982 0286 3 (hardback)
978 1 3982 0285 6 (paperback)

British Library Cataloguing in Publication Data
A full catalogue record for this book is available from the British Library.

Acknowledgements
Capstone Press/Karon Dubke, 20; Getty Images/Bettmann, 19; iStockphoto: andresr, 4, Andyworks, 11; Capstone Press/Karon Dubke, 12, 20; Dreamstime/Petar Dojkic, 5; Getty Images: Andrea Booher/FEMA/Handout, 11, Hulton Archive/Stringer, 18; iStockphoto/dstephens, 4; Newscom/Gerard Lacz/VWPics, 13; Shutterstock: 135pixels, 15, DTeibe Photography, 17, Grigorita Ko, 7, Jagodka, cover, Kachalkina Veronika, 9, Katarzyna Mazurowska, 8, Nature Art, cover (bottom), Osetrik, 16, Photo Melon, back cover
Artistic elements: Shutterstock: Anbel, Miloje

Every effort has been made to contact copyright holders of material reproduced in this book. Any omissions will be rectified in subsequent printings if notice is given to the publisher.

All the internet addresses (URLs) given in this book were valid at the time of going to press. However, due to the dynamic nature of the internet, some addresses may have changed, or sites may have changed or ceased to exist since publication. While the author and publisher regret any inconvenience this may cause readers, no responsibility for any such changes can be accepted by either the author or the publisher.

Printed and bound in India

Contents

The faithful German shepherd 4
German shepherd history 8
A hard worker 10
Keeping German shepherds healthy 14
Caring for a German shepherd 16
Fun facts about German shepherds 18
    Make a tug-of-war dog toy 20
    Glossary 22
    Find out more 23
    Websites 23
    Index 24

Words in **bold** are in the glossary.

The faithful German shepherd

German shepherds are very **popular** dogs. They are clever and loyal. They love to be with their owners.

Woof! German shepherds bark at strangers. They want to keep their families safe. The faithful German shepherd makes a wonderful pet.

German shepherds can be a mix of colours. Most shepherds have black and light brown fur. Shepherds have a **double coat**. The bottom coat is soft. The hairs are close together. Longer fur covers this coat.

German shepherds are big dogs. They weigh 23 to 41 kilograms (50 to 90 pounds). They stand 56 to 66 centimetres (22 to 26 inches) tall. Shepherds have pointed ears. They have large heads.

German shepherd history

The first German shepherds lived in Germany in the 1800s. These dogs were made to be clever and strong. They **herded** sheep.

In the 1900s, shepherds became popular around the world. Today, they belong to the herding group of dogs. Shepherds run and jump in contests. Some still herd sheep.

A hard worker

German shepherds are hard workers. They make great search and **rescue** dogs. Shepherds jump into action when people are lost or hurt. They have a strong sense of smell. They find people by following scents. Shepherds don't give up. They save lives.

German shepherds do many other jobs too. Some shepherds work as police dogs. They begin police training at 1 year old. These dogs help keep people safe.

12

German shepherds also help people who are blind. A **guide dog** wears a special harness. Its owner holds the harness. German shepherds lead their owners around safely.

Keeping German shepherds healthy

Most German shepherds are healthy. They should visit a **vet** once a year. A vet makes sure dogs stay healthy. A vet will check a dog's heart and lungs. She will look at its eyes and ears too. German shepherds live for about 10 years.

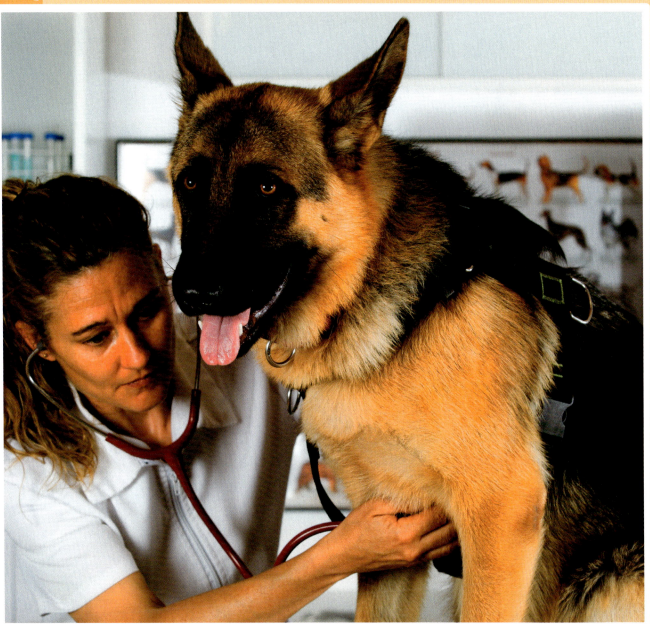

Caring for a German shepherd

German shepherds have lots of **energy**! They need daily **exercise**. Most German shepherds aren't messy dogs. But they do shed a lot. They should be brushed weekly.

German shepherds love to learn. They are easy to train. Puppies should be trained early. Let your German shepherd puppy meet new people. Take your puppy to new places.

Fun facts about German shepherds

- A German shepherd called Rin-Tin-Tin was famous. He starred in more than 25 films.

- The first guide dogs were German shepherds.

- German shepherds were used in World War I to carry messages and to help rescue people.

- Shepherds do not like very hot weather.

- Some people call German shepherds German "shedders".

Make a tug-of-war dog toy

What you need:

- scissors
- two old towels

What you do:

1. Cut a towel into three large strips. Each strip should be about 5 cm (2 inches) wide. It should be at least 38 cm (15 inches) long.

2. Cut a towel into two small strips. Each strip should be about 3 cm (1 inch) wide. It should be about 28 cm (11 inches) long.

3. Place the three large strips together. Use a small strip to tie them together at one end. Then plait the three large strips together. Use the last small strip to tie off the other end.

4. Play tug-of-war with your German shepherd!

Glossary

double coat a coat that is thick and soft close to the skin and covered with lighter, silky fur on the surface

energy the strength to do active things without getting tired

exercise a physical activity done in order to stay healthy and fit

guide dog a dog that is specially trained to lead people who are blind

herd to round up animals, such as sheep, and keep them together

popular liked or enjoyed by many people

rescue to save someone who is in danger

vet a doctor trained to take care of animals

Find out more

Amazing Dogs, Laura Buller (DK Children, 2016)

Looking After Dogs and Puppies (Pet Guides), Katherine Starke (Usborne, 2013)

Totally Amazing Facts About Dogs (Mind Benders), Nikki Potts (Raintree, 2019)

Websites

German Shepherd Dog
www.ducksters.com/animals/german_shepherd.php

The Kennel Club: German Shepherd Dog
www.thekennelclub.org.uk/search/breeds-a-to-z/breeds/pastoral/german-shepherd-dog/

Index

barking 5
body parts 6

care 14, 16–17

exercise 16

fur 6, 16, 19

guide dogs 13, 19

herding 8, 9
history 8–9

police dogs 12

rescue dogs 10

size 6

training 12, 17